THIRTEEN CENTURIES OF

ENGLISH

CHURCH MUSIC

An Introduction
to a Great National Tradition

by

W. H. PARRY

HINRICHSEN EDITION LIMITED

25 *Museum Street, London, W.C.*1

228625

First Edition, July, 1946

Second (enlarged) Edition, November, 1946

For

E.M. & S.P.

Made and Printed in Great Britain by
CLARIDGE, LEWIS AND JORDAN LTD.
68 Wardour Street, London, W.1

AUTHOR'S NOTE

It is difficult, in compiling a brief historical outline of a subject, to avoid saying much that has been said before—for one is tied to the essential and often the obvious, facts. It is equally difficult therefore to acknowledge any extraneous sources of information that may occur. Concerning the present work, certainly most of the authors mentioned in the bibliography must have had some influence, together with others whom, through the hiatus of war-service, the writer has forgotten.

If this little book succeeds in providing an easy and accessible introduction to the subject, and in enlarging the general interest in Church Music, it is hoped that any indirect contributor will accept the thanks of both author and reader.

I take the opportunity of expressing sincere thanks to Dr. R. Vaughan Williams, O.M., and Mr. Inglis Gundry, for reading the MS. of the historical survey and making valuable suggestions.

The portraits of John Blow, Henry Purcell and William Boyce are reproduced respectively from "Amphion Anglicus" (1700), "Orpheus Britannicus" (1698) and Boyce's "Cathedral Music" Vol. I, 2nd edition, copies having been kindly loaned for the purpose by H. Watkins Shaw, Esq.

The following publishers have kindly granted permission for musical extracts to be reproduced:

Messrs. BOSWORTH: *W. Crotch*: Comfort, O Lord (No. 4)

Messrs. CURWEN:
R. Vaughan Williams: Let us now praise famous men
R. R. Terry: Myn Lyking (No. 89008)

OXFORD UNIVERSITY PRESS (Tudor Church Music):
Orlando Gibbons: Almighty and everlasting God (No. 36)
Thomas Weelkes: Gloria in Excelsis (No. 17)

Messrs. NOVELLO:
Thomas Attwood: Turn Thy Face (Musical Times Series)
S. Wesley: In Exitu Israel (No. 348)
S. S. Wesley: Thou wilt keep him (No. 107)
Purcell: Service in G minor (No. 852)
Walmisley: Service in D minor (No. 46)

Messrs. DEANE & SONS:
C. Hubert H. Parry: My soul, there is a country

W. H. P.

CONTENTS

THIRTEEN CENTURIES OF
ENGLISH CHURCH MUSIC

By W. H. PARRY

I. INTRODUCTION

An increasing number of people are becoming aware that Britain is not, after all, a country without music. Many have vaguely heard, too, that England once had a "golden age" of music when she was the leader of the art in Europe —as some claim her to be to-day.

Britain's musical achievements have in fact been very considerable, and throughout our history we have been greatly indebted to the Church, which possesses a fine wealth of the most beautiful music : a heritage which is far less widely known than it deserves.

Admittedly it is difficult to know church music unless one experiences it in its proper setting—in fact unless one goes to church ! And even then one must be fortunate or discriminating in one's choice, for the mere weekly round of hymns and psalms which many churches still provide is but a minute part of this subject. Like all music to-day, however, it is available for enjoyment at home—through cheap publications, the gramophone, and the wireless.

As throughout its long history, it is no small part of the church's musical value that it provides the most easily accessible form of music for the amateur to participate in. It provides a fine training-ground for the appreciation of all forms of music—and the writer makes no secret of his hopes that some readers of this brief work may become tempted to join actively in the present-day performances of church music.

This book then, is intended for three types of readers :

1. The musically-minded person who hitherto has missed this whole branch of the musical art, regarding music as something essentially of the concert-hall.

2. The organ-student or chorister who is so fortunate as to be an executive of this music.

3. The general reader who is interested in the cultural history of his country.

Before approaching the history of church music—that is, music written expressly for church and cathedral services —we must briefly consider one fundamental question. **Why has music always been associated with religious ceremony ?**

In outline the answer is this. Music is the most intangible of the arts, being beyond all contact with the material world. The sculptor and the painter depict tangible objects : the architect is bound by the utilitarian demands of his building and by the law of gravity : the poet is constantly striving to overcome the bonds which cumbersome words set on his flights of thought. All these artists have, within their limitations, added to the glory of English church tradition. But the musician is completely free. If we try to analyse his work we become aware of his craftsmanship, it is true, but the mystery of the composer's power remains. All we can say is that the music has an effect on us—and beyond that its function almost defies investigation. Psychologists state that music can satisfy our "herd instinct." In the mere sing-song of people at a party, or the vast chorus of a football crowd, we say that a powerful "atmosphere" is created. With religious music however this "atmosphere" is raised to its purest and highest plane, and music can transcend us to realms of spiritual receptiveness.

This invaluable power has always been recognised by leaders of religion : and indeed, on surveying the history of the church, one is tempted to conclude that whenever the church's power and influence were at their height, its music too was very flourishing—and this was part of the cause rather than the effect !

In order to examine church music adequately, the reader must be introduced to much early music which he is never likely to hear. However, no apology is made for this, because it will be found to be — even in the brief study possible here—a fascinating chapter of history, and one which will add interest and colour to his outlook on music generally. The chief aim has been to trace the continuous development of our church music, and in so small a space many worthy names have been omitted in the interests of clarity. The reader, should he be inclined, is advised to investigate the subject further—for which end the bibliography will be of great assistance.

He will learn most of all, however, from the music itself, and works recommended for study (costing a few pence each) are listed at the close of the chapters.

II. THE FOUNDATIONS (A.D. 600—1,000)

The origin of music, as a source of expression and delight, probably lies soon after the time when man emerged from pure animal status—when his instincts began to become controllable emotions, and when dawning intellect stirred him to create his own delights to satisfy these emotions.

What actually occurred in music prior to its association with the Christian Church in Britain is a matter chiefly for speculation, and is beyond the scope of the present work. However, it is important for our purpose to realise that both voices and instruments had been combined in ritual, entertainment, and dancing, for some thousands of years. We know this from biblical references alone. But when several instruments play together a degree of harmonisation is implied : and when music accompanies the dance, a sense of metrical rhythm is inevitable. Music then had some degree of organisation—although all this is veiled from us by the loss, where any existed, of written records.

Britain too must have had her share of this pagan music for centuries, but music as an art in this country began at the close of the sixth century, with the introduction of music to the Christian Church.

MUSIC OF THE SEVENTH CENTURY

At this point our best approach to this mere essence of English music is to discover what it was not, and how it differed from the music we hear to-day.

1. It had no "time" and no "harmony." Thus the simplest of our modern hymn-tunes would be wildly incomprehensible to a seventh-century singer.

2. Implied by the above, it had no sense of phrase-lengths, or of modulation to different keys.

3. It was purely vocal music, having no accompaniment : none of our modern instruments were then invented.

4. It could not be written down because our system of notation, too, had not been invented.

5. It was what we can generalise as Roman Catholic music, and all the texts were in Latin. There was, of course, no Church of England as we know it to-day.

THREE GREAT EVENTS OF THE SEVENTH CENTURY

I. The introduction of Plainsong with its modal scales.

Plainsong was introduced by Aethelbert, King of Kent, just before the end of the sixth century, and St. Augustine, who brought it with him from Rome, became the first archbishop of Canterbury (and thus the founder of English music).

II. Development of Neums.

Neums, a primitive system of notation, came into use not long afterwards, obviously as a result of the expansion of plainsong in the church ritual.

III. The church, the only seat of learning in the land, became the centre of the musical art, giving music indeed the right to be called an art. As mentioned above, we do not know what secular music existed at the dawn of the church tradition, but it is most probable that the purpose and discipline with which the church imbued music—while giving it a healthy and careful cultivation—restricted it from many desirable advances which occurred outside : advances which the church recognised and adopted often with much reluctance. For centuries the church laboriously cultivated its music while the songs of the countryside grew profusely and at will.

Let us glance then at the main feature of plainsong, modes, and neums.

Plainsong

The name is important in that it implied a reaction to music that was ornamented (and which we have said, must have existed in secular society). It is an appropriate term too, for this was music at its plainest. It was a kind of elevated speech to a simple melody (called a *canto fermo*), with a basic reciting-note around which it moved. Later it developed an intricate vocal art around these "cantos" (*canto fermo* means "fixed song"), but for congregational use in psalms and responses it can still be heard in something like its original form—although, of course, it is now accompanied by the organ, as a rule. With its simple unison melodies and "speech-rhythm" structure it was ideally suitable for congregational singing.

(As the system developed the *canto* was sung by the tenors, who had to hold on to this melody while others sang different notes. Hence the term "tenor"—from the Latin *tenere*—"to hold on").

Pure plainsong found its peak of achievement in the early eleventh century, after which new forces were at work.

Modes

Modal scales provided the musical material for plainsong, and, indeed, for all music until our present scales emerged at the end of the seventeenth century.

Our modern (diatonic) scales are all transpositions of a standard pattern : *e.g.,* in major scales, the semitones occur invariably between the third and fourth, and seventh and eighth notes; thus to every major scale we can sing our doh ray me fah soh lah te doh formula. However, let the reader play on the piano the white notes from middle D, for an octave, and try to sing the sol-fa scale. This is obviously something very different. It has the semitones at different points—and is, in fact, probably the oldest scale in our western civilisation. It is the Dorian Mode, by far the most popular scale of this period.

St. Ambrose, Bishop of Milan, established four modes for church use in the fourth century. They were, in white notes on the piano:

Dorian	...	...	...	D to D
Phrygian	...	...	...	E to E
Lydian	...	...	...	F to F
Mixolydian	...	...	...	G to G

Each of these scales, it can be seen, contains a different arrangement of semitones, and consequently sounds different — even when transposed in pitch, as they frequently were. (The " reciting-note " which we have mentioned was almost invariably the fifth note of these scales: it dominated the music, and thus the fifth became known as the "dominant" of any scale).

Pope Gregory, before sending St. Augustine to this country, established four new modes on the dominants of the original four, and with these eight modes the system was complete up to the sixteenth century—when four more were added.

Some important points concerning the modal system

I. There was tremendous scope for variety of sound in a system with so many scales. We do not appreciate how completely the modern diatonic scale has become part of us, until we hear the effect of different scales, such as these modes—or, to quote an extreme case, those of Arabic music.

II. The "reciting-note" used to resolve on to the root (*i.e.*, the doh) of the scale, and this was the germ of harmony, developing a sense of relative pitch and cadence.

Neums (or Neumes) : the slow growth of a musical script

A brief review of the growth of musical script must find its place here for several reasons :

1. It throws considerable light on the music of the times.

2. It is essentially a product of church music.

3. A highly developed form of the early system is still in wide use in church plainsong-manuals.

One of the reasons that music has lagged behind its fellow arts is that it was so long finding a written medium. An individual genius would die, and apart from what his pupils remembered, nothing could be "handed down." Composers were practical experimenters. They were well aware, however, for the need for notation, for countless experiments were made from the earliest days of English music.

From such attempts developed the system of neums. It looked rather like our present-day shorthand, and was scrawled above the text to show the rise and fall of the music. With some limitations it reached a high degree of competence, although, like all primitive "languages," it became unduly complex.

The chief among its limitations were :

(a) It did not indicate the exact extent of the rise and fall, and consequently there was a considerable amount of guess-work needed.

(b) There was no standard system, many writers using their own peculiar versions. Thus manuscripts were not widely inter-changeable.

(c) It could not give the relative length of notes. This was not a great disadvantage in music that depended so much on the rhythm of the words.

We must look ahead to the tenth century for the next development, which reached the valuable goal of being a system from which one could read music at sight. It was

a system of "notation" — using notes in the following
manner :

semi-breve	black diamond
breve	black square
long	breve with a stem
maxima	black rectangle (double square) and stem

while later were added

minima	semi-breve with a stem
semi-minima	minima with a stem and a tail (like our present quaver)

Obviously here is the origin of our modern notation—
for it only remained for some of the shapes not to
be "blacked in" for our modern semi-breves, minims, etc.,
to emerge. This stage was not reached for several centuries
and meanwhile many trials were made with coloured notes,
etc., to deal with the growing complexity of the music. The
problem of relative time-values was not yet solved either, for
the maxima could equal two or three breves according to
its context in the music.

Originating in the tenth century too, was the other great
invention : the use of lines to indicate the exact rise and
fall of the music.

Starting with one line, the system eventually resulted
with four—as it has to-day in our plainsong-manuals. Here
again various colours were used at first to distinguish the
lines, and it is interesting that the early exponents of this
system regarded it merely as a teaching-method for new
music—to be discarded as soon as possible by the learner.
Presumably it made music too easy !

The clef, a K-shaped sign—really a C—appeared fairly
early to fix the root of the scale, but time-signatures did not
appear until the fifteenth century, and such refinements as
bar-lines until about 1600.

Nevertheless, by the time our Magna Carta was signed,
music was well on the way towards having a written
language !

III. CHURCH MUSIC ADVANCES (1000—1400)

The year 1000 is probably rather early to mark this second stage in church music. However, a great deal of deductive guess-work must be employed in these initial centuries, and the date is temptingly convenient. Music was of course advancing from its very inception, but some vital changes began to take place about this time which greatly accelerated the process.

1. Organum—The Beginning of Harmony

Up to the tenth century all church music had been in unison—or where soprano voices were used, in octaves. The way this was superceded is curious in the extreme, and probably was due to the lack of musical sense rather than the development of it.

When the plainsong *canto fermo* was sung, it was pitched (by the priest) at some mid-way point in the voice-span, *e.g.*, A or G. But many tenors and basses would find the *canto* far more comfortable to sing at the mid-way point of their *own* voice-span. Thus the practice crept in of singing parallel parts to the *canto* at intervals of a fourth above and a fifth below; which means, of course, singing the melody at the root-notes of the scale as well as at the dominant.

If then the sopranos sang the *canto* an octave higher than the original pitch we now have a kind of four-part harmony—except that all the parts were singing the same tune : and the effect of this curious parallel music, as is often pointed out, may not have been as unpleasant as we at first imagine. (The greater number would be singing the original *canto* tones). It is, in fact, an effect occasionally reclaimed by some of our modern English composers.

The challenge to loosen the bonds of parallel organum was at first met in the following ways :

(*a*) The gradual introduction of thirds and sixths among the organum fourths and fifths.

These new intervals made their appearance at the end of the thirteenth century. (It is amazing that the simple third—a doh-me chord of two notes, was considered barbarous and revolutionary for so long).

(b) The use of passing-notes.

If two consecutive notes in a melody were a third apart, there was a tendency to join them up by means of an intermediate note.

(c) The influence of descant composers who experimented with a canto and one other free part.

A fair stage of harmonic advancement was attained by the late fourteenth century. And after harmonising a *canto* fairly freely with three other parts it only remained for the composer to invent his own *canto* for true harmonic composition to begin.

2. Polyphony

Polyphony (which we can identify with counterpoint) is a tremendous advance on the old organum : for whereas in the previous system the voice-parts were strictly parallel, polyphony meant independence of parts — and from the eleventh century onwards the polyphonic age slowly increased in skill and maturity.

Among the chief contributions to its advancement were :

(a) The combining of several established melodies.

This peculiar practice was quite common, the melodies being slightly modified where they clashed badly. Frequently each melody retained its original words !

(b) Imitation.

It was found a pleasurable experience for one voice-part to repeat a phrase immediately after another. This had the valuable effect of giving each part prominence in turn, a vast advance on the old *canto* idea.

(c) Contrary motion and the crossing of parts.

Parts moving in contrary motion were found to establish a feeling of symmetry. The crossing of vocal lines was another important step towards freedom.

(*d*) The introduction of "rests."

A part entering after a series of rests did so with the effect of emphasis, and added to the independent importance of the polyphonic strands.

All the above, too, contributed to the expansion of harmony—for when the parts moved freely, the harmonic chords through which they moved (*i.e.*, the vertical cross-section of this lateral movement) naturally varied a great deal. The greatest problem of composers at this time was to write attractive independent parts which did not produce unpleasant harmonic clashes with others.

By the end of this second preparatory period polyphony had become the established medium for the church Mass, although of course it still had much to learn. Sense of metrical time and of "relative keys" was slow to come. We now expect music to be based on a regular rhythmical pattern, and also that it should "modulate" to various keys —to give it a satisfying form. Whether we are technically aware of these things or not we would miss their presence in early polyphony, finding it aimless and restless. It was for the great early English composers to overcome these deficiencies.

At this stage we are first in contact with one of the chief problems of church music. Music was becoming a complex art which could be performed only by an educated minority, and what music gained in artistic achievement the church often lost in the fervour of the congregation. There were, however, considerable "congregational" parts of the service, such as psalms and responses; early hymns were now beginning to appear, too, with their short simple phrases and more regular metre.

3. *Instrumental Accompaniments*

Even in such a brief background to church music a glance must be made at accompaniments, which became almost universal in this period.

Organs were certainly in use in this country in the ninth century. But for several centuries the organist's post was not so much one for a musician as for the strongest man available! Organs at first had draw-bars to release the wind into the pipes, but soon adopted keys—about fifteen in all, about four inches wide, and played (of necessity) with the fist. When organs began to grow to size, it frequently took forty or fifty blowers, working treddle-bellows to supply the wind. Reed pipes were not introduced until the late fifteenth century, and pedals not for three hundred years after that. No doubt, however, these early organs served admirably in supporting the simple *canto* of church plain-song.

Viols, resembling violins and 'cellos, had a prominent place in church music, playing the same music as the voice-parts.

Other instruments : it would appear from contemporary records that most of the instruments exalted in the 150th Psalm—including the "loud cymbals"—found their way into church accompaniments, much to the distress of many dignitaries of the twelfth and thirteenth centuries. Secular influences have always presented a problem for those concerned with church music!

Altogether the services of these early centuries must have made a very joyful noise—which, of course, does not in any way reflect on their sincerity and fervour.

4. *Institutions*

Music could not spread and advance without organised centres of development. At first the church provided these alone. The seed of plainsong planted at Canterbury was to flourish in cathedrals, churches, abbeys, and monasteries throughout the land. But in the middle of the twelfth century the *Chapel Royal* was founded as a court institution for all musical purposes. It soon became the leading influence when kings began to vie with foreign monarchs in the excellence of their music. An interesting feature was the "press-gang" system established by Richard III, whereby choristers from other institutions could be legitimately "stolen" for service at court. This licence was wisely used however, and no doubt the choir-boys concerned raised few objections.

Most of our greatest composers were "Gentlemen of the Chapel," and the enthusiastic patronage of monarchs,

A tenth century organ

and an organ of the thirteenth century

especially the Tudors, was invaluable to musical development.

Up to about 1400 then, church music was slow and laborious in its growth. By our present standards it lacked variety and expression : it was vague and unmeasured : any music of this early period would sound harsh and almost incoherent to us to-day.

A Note on Recorded Music

The "Columbia History of Music" and the Parlophone "Two Thousand Years of Music" contain numerous interesting examples of Continental church music of ensuing centuries, together with some English secular works by composers we are to mention. Unfortunately recordings of English church music of these periods are very rare, but when they occur they are mentioned at the end of the relevant chapters.

Pertaining to the present chapter, the reader's attention is drawn to a record of plainsong with organum and with descant (Columbia 5710).

IV. THE FIFTEENTH CENTURY— SOME EARLY NAMES

Music in its early stages was inevitably regarded as a science, and there was nothing of our modern "artistic" conception about it. It was a jig-saw puzzle of fitting notes together—a matter of mechanical ingenuity. Theorists were then more plentiful than composers, and passing reference must be made to JOHN OF SALISBURY, a close friend of Thomas à Becket, whose "De Arte Musices" as early as 1200 had shown a surprising knowledge of the polyphonic problems we have been discussing.

The first great executive name in English music however was JOHN DUNSTABLE, who died in 1458, and at this initial point in church music history it is clear that Britain possessed the leading composer in Europe. His greatness lay in the composing, chiefly in three parts, of fluent contrapuntal music, and in the avoidance of those harmonic clashes which were the bane of lesser polyphonic writers.

We have little of his music available to-day, but pupils coming to him from the continent set in motion the great Netherlands schools of musical composition. Exchange of knowledge was very free in this age, and the profound influence Dunstable had on European music was returned about a century later. The continental composers advanced quickly, and one of the developments they brought back with them was the *Motet* (roughly what we would call an anthem).

The value of the motet was soon apparent to English musicians, for it gave a wide choice of texts for musical settings. The formal Mass was naturally a restricted medium—and tended to become tied to its plainsong origins, but the motet encouraged composers to make their music more widely and more personally expressive. The motet-form had found its way into this country before the end of the fifteenth century.

Although the century was a quiet one after Dunstable's death, there were several composers whose names are still recalled, and—fortunately—whose music can still be heard. FAYRFAX, who died in 1521, had been a worthy contemporary of Dunstable, and later in the century came REDFORD, SHEPPARD, and CORNYSHE—all of whom helped to lay the foundations for the wonderful work of their successors. Their chief value lay in increased ease and fluency of part-writing. Music was becoming less of an ingenious and laborious science.

Some Music of the Fifteenth Century

Probably the earliest English anthems in use to-day are SHEPPARD'S *Haste thee, O God*, and REDFORD'S *Rejoice in the Lord*. (Novello.)

There is also a *Magnificat and Nunc Dimittis* attributed to FAYRFAX.

Our practical acquaintance with DUNSTABLE should increase as a result of present-day research. Many fragments of music, both sacred and secular, are tentatively attributed to him, but obscurities in the writing of the manuscripts are a great hindrance.

V. THE SIXTEENTH CENTURY—THE
REFORMATION—TUDOR COMPOSERS

This century showed the first full flower of English music, and almost a score of fine composers of the period are heard today. Advance now became rapid, helped additionally by the introduction of music-printing about 1500.

Some important General Features of the Age:

1. The solving of polyphonic problems led to freedom of expression; music became more varied, and even descriptive.

2. Secular music diverged from church music, and instrumental from vocal music.

3. Sense of time and key developed: our diatonic scale was closely approached.

4. As the purely secular forms developed, they influenced church music, giving it a new vitality.

5. English music was again the leading influence on the Continent.

Among several fine composers at the beginning of the century was TAVERNER (died 1543) and names ever-growing in stature followed. His choice of the secular "O Western Wind," upon which to base a Mass, is a significant breach in tradition, showing the desire in composers to increase expression, individuality, and naturalness.

CHRISTOPHER TYE, born about 1500, was the "father" of a long line of great composers. His greatest personal contribution was in the development of the motet, where he showed distinct power of personal expression, and an aptness of music to the words. Like Taverner, he is notable for his use of secular folk-song as the *canto* for Masses. There is still something of the scientific and academic flavour about his work, but he can show much of the grace and ease of his renowned pupils whose names follow. He could write freely and naturally in six parts.

Thomas Tallis (1515-1585)

Tallis is the greatest composer to date. His name is well known through the wide present use of his Versicles and Responses, in which he harmonised the traditional plain-song: also, of course, for his eternally-loved hymn-tune, *"Tallis' Canon"* ("Glory to thee my God this night"). He wrote a *"Song of Forty Parts"* as a rejoiner to a Continental virtuoso-piece of thirty-six, and this shows, at any rate, the degree of facility which had been reached in polyphonic writing. Tallis is in few respects inferior to his more lauded contemporary Palestrina (died 1594) and a large number of his anthems and service-settings are still frequently heard. His works show surprising advances in variety and subtlety of expression, as well as great skill in the imitative treatment of the voice-parts.

The Tallis Canon

The Reformation—An Interruption in Tradition

In the midst of this great musical activity came Henry VIII's factions with the Pope, and their subsequent revolutionary effects on the English Church.

The three largest musical factors were :

(A) The dissolution of the monasteries (1536-9). This was an undoubted set-back for music, curtailing the activities of many valuable musicians. King Henry's love of music tempered the blow however, for many of the leading composers (e.g., Tallis, at Waltham Abbey) found a place in the Chapel Royal. The Cathedral music remained undisturbed.

(B) The first English Prayer Book. The Anglicising of the church services was of greater effect. The traditional Latin Masses had to be adapted to English or discarded —as too the earlier motets. Also composers now had the new problem of writing for the English tongue. In the long run, however, the change was an excellent thing :

It led to a more "national" music.

It brought the music nearer to the common people. English, with its more virile structure, had greater possibilities for rhythmic and expressive composition.

Composers of the century were well equal to the challenge and JOHN MERBECKE (died 1585) issued his *"Boke of Common Prayer Noted"* (i.e., set to music) within twelve months of the Prayer Book being issued. He used the ancient plainsong to the English words, and showed that the new simpler Communion Service could be successfully set in the English tongue. This work is still in wide use.

(c) The outcry for simplification by the Protestants. This third element of the Reformation appeared quite as disturbing as the others, but, fortunately, it proved that the Protestants were not to achieve such power as their Lutheran counterparts—who swept away previous styles for a simple note-for-syllable method. Tallis, Tye, and others, experimented with simple chordal music as opposed to the intricate older Masses, but the eventual result was that the old style kept its place— often tempered by a refreshing harmonic simplicity.

A very notable result of the Reformation's simplifying influence was the impetus given to Anglican chanting of the psalms and to the singing of hymns.

The hymn form was as old as plainsong itself but its use was not extensive until the present period. In its English form it grew from the singing of metrical psalms—psalms paraphrased to regular verse-patterns, thus allowing a single symmetrical tune to serve for all verses without the need of reciting notes. Several famous collections of these hymns, led by that of Sternhold, Hopkins and Day, in 1562, achieved very widespread popularity. Strongly influenced by plainsong, they retained the melody in the tenor part—and it was almost a century later that the present form of hymn with the melody in the treble was finally established. In the matter of hymn-singing the English Church has always been much indebted to non-conformist invention, and the Scottish influence beginning at this period is typical.

Anglican chanting was a development of the now harmonised (Gregorian) plainsong, and was more musically balanced in keeping with the trend of the times. It is from this period that the formal composition of chants began, as opposed to the mere adaptation of old plainsong melodies to Anglican use. The double chant, so common in all our churches today was essentially a product of the next century, as was our established system of "pointing." Our present method, although envisaged in Reformation times, was hindered in its development by a falling away of choral singing in the churches. It was, in fact, a cathedral product, and congregational psalm-singing did not reach its present status in the normal church service until the nineteenth century.

Having briefly reviewed the chief effects and implications of the Reformation, we can now return to those composers whose work it immediately affected.

RICHARD FARRANT (died 1580)

Farrant, another really great composer, showed the simplifying influence of the Reformation in his church compositions, and his anthems and service-settings are still a joy to hear in our churches. His work is more "modern" in flavour than his predecessors, lacking only some developments in modulation and metrical rhythm. What it lacks from our modern standards, however, gives it a charm and grace which modern composers rarely achieve.

WILLIAM BYRD (1543-1623)

Unlike Tallis, his teacher—who was a complete specialist in church music—Byrd wrote in many styles and many forms. Secular music was now gaining sway in the country, and Byrd became the leader of the new Madrigal and keyboard schools of composition. He was certainly as great as any Continental contemporary, and showed great advances in the expressiveness and appropriateness of his music. Composition was now showing distinct signs of conveying deep personal feeling. Byrd, retaining the Catholic Faith, loved the old music, and devoted part of his time to the writing of Masses—although, of course, they could never be sung publicly. They are still available to us today, however.

At the close of the century it was secular music, especially the madrigal, which was the chief concern of composers' minds. MORLEY, DOWLAND, BEVIN and WEELKES are typical of this great secular school, although their church music is still frequently heard. They are all worthy companions of Byrd. THOMAS TOMKINS was notable for introducing solo parts into anthems, while JOHN BULL (a kind of minor Handel in his expansiveness and varied interests) showed distinct harmonic advances in his church compositions.

Some Music of the Sixteenth Century

Taverner :	Christe Jesu	Oxford
Tye :	O Come, ye servants of the Lord	Novello
	Sing to the Lord	Novello
	Magnificat and Nunc Dimittis in G minor	Novello
Farrant :	Call to remembrance	Oxford
	Kyrie Eleison in G minor	Novello
Tallis :	O nata lux	Oxford
	Salvator mundi	Oxford
	O Sacrum Convivium	Stainer & Bell
Byrd :	Ave Verum	Oxford
	Sing joyfully unto God	Novello
	Bow Thine ear, O Lord	Novello
Dowland :	Come, Holy Ghost	Novello
Tomkins :	Magnificat and Nunc Dimittis in C	Novello
Weelkes :	Gloria in Excelsis	Oxford
	O how amiable	Oxford
King Henry VIII : (or Munday)	O Lord, the maker of all thing	Novello

Some Recordings

Tye :	O Come, ye servants of the Lord	H.M.V. RG 8
Byrd :	Creed, from "Short Service"	H.M.V. RG 4
Byrd :	Sanctus, from Mass for five voices	H.M.V. RG 11

VI. THE SEVENTEENTH CENTURY—THE COMMONWEALTH AND RESTORATION

With Italy, England now led the world in secular music, and composers were not so specifically interested in the church as they had been previously.

One great man however devoted much of his varied genius to church composition :

ORLANDO GIBBONS (1585–1625)

Gibbons showed perfect adaptation of the old polyphonic style to the simplified Anglican service. As is frequently said, he stands out as his greater contemporary Shakespeare did in the field of letters. He seized, co-ordinated, and exploited all the forces available to him, and gave a vigorous fresh impetus to religious music. (He could not be musical "Shakespeare" of course, because for all its advancement music was still a limited and immature art. Shakespeare had the full resources of the English tongue at his command, and his range, depth, and craftsmanship have never been surpassed). Gibbons, nevertheless, was the climax of the whole church tradition, and very many of his anthems and service-settings have never been equalled in their particular medium.

BENJAMIN ROGERS and ADRIAN BATTEN were two very progressive composers carrying on the Gibbons tradition until the Commonwealth disrupted the whole art. They are notable for further advances in harmonic sense and phrase-structure, and for the use of bar-lines in the modern manner.

The musical art as a whole however had passed its present peak by the time of Gibbon's death.

The Commonwealth (1649-1660)
—the second interruption in tradition

Cromwell's attitude to music was the recurrent one—in an extreme form—of simplification. Cromwell himself was a lover of music, even having his own official organist; and the wholesale destruction of music and organs is usually held to be the work of his more fanatical subordinates—in their hatred for "superstitious ornaments" and anything resembling "Popery." Apart from the material losses in music, the Commonwealth shattered the musical tradition. By the time of the Restoration most of the leaders had died, and no younger generation had been taught—the cathedral choir-schools and the Chapel Royal were empty in this period. Consequently in 1660 the churches literally did not know how to begin in restoring the old traditions.

The Restoration

Charles II had spent his exile in France, where his undisciplined and superficial character had tasted the showy splendours of Louis XIV's court : splendours which he was determined to equal in England. He straightway sent a very promising young musician, PELHAM HUMPHREY, to study the gay secular French music—of which LULLY was now becoming the leader. Humphrey returned to lead a new burst of musical activity, which, with the old musical institutions fully restored and the enthusiasm of the king, developed rapidly.

(Pelham Humphrey's name is immortal in English music for what must be one of the simplest—yet very appropriate and artistic—compositions of all time, his single chant for the 150th Psalm. The new conditions and philosophy of this age led to a more widespread use of Anglican chanting, as well as to a strong and worthy growth of English hymn-writing).

As we may expect, however, the general reflection of all these historic events on church music was very considerable.

The break in tradition had made the old polyphonic scholarship a thing of the past, and these strong secular influences gave church composition a new and less solemn flavour, as well as a far wider range of thought and expression. Altogether then, as with the previous severing of the tradition in Reformation days, the events proved more of a blessing than otherwise, especially as it appeared that Gibbons had exhausted the possibilities of the old polyphony. The new music was set firmly in the direction of our modern, more harmonic, compositions.

MICHAEL WISE (born 1648) and JOHN BLOW (born in 1649) became the leaders of the new school and their works are still frequently heard. The newer art is not mature yet however and they lack some of the freedom and facility of earlier writers, although showing advances in personal expression.

In the next great name however, we see English music once again a flourishing and polished art—and of strong international influence. We have mentioned that people refer to a golden age of English music: they have in mind the Elizabethan era. **English music had, in fact, one long golden age for two whole centuries, with its peaks of achievement at Dunstable, Byrd, Gibbons, and now finally—out-topping the others—Purcell.**

HENRY PURCELL (1658-1695)

Purcell, a pupil of Blow, fulfilled a similar function to the earlier Byrd and Gibbons in that he grasped—in his short life—all opportunities and possibilities of his time, and showed an amazing maturity in all known forms of musical composition. For this reason he is frequently compared with Mozart. It is fruitless to speculate, but one is tempted to ponder what may have happened if Purcell had lived a normal span—or for that matter if he had been born a century later with a Haydn to precede him. He remains nevertheless a very great genius.

His anthems, of which over fifty are still sung, showed a perfect fusion of the secular ayre (*i.e.*, solo song) with the traditional motet. But it is in his great facility and variety of expression that his true greatness lies : stateliness, solemnity, poignancy, tenderness, all found their full place, as well as a livelier jollity which was more in keeping with the times. His magnificent *Te Deum in D* for voices, organ, strings, and trumpets, is a great monument in English music, and epitomises all that is best in Restoration composition. At the same time however, he could write such an anthem as *Let my prayer come up into Thy Presence*—tender, delicate, and pleading, with a wealth of harmonic beauty worthy of J. S. Bach : the work of a man who felt subtly and deeply, and who could express his feeling in music with complete freedom. These works, although not yet in our present-day idiom, are completely satisfying to the modern ear, and in their aims have never been more successfully accomplished.

The more one considers the extravagance, laxity, and shallow superficiality of the Restoration period the more amazing do Purcell's achievements become, both in sacred and secular music. But despite his mastery of the newer developments in harmony and rhythm, he was steeped in the scholarly old polyphonic tradition—a fact for which we must be profoundly thankful.

A number of contemporaries, too, must not be forgotten in the glory of a greater man, JEREMIAH CLARKE (died 1707) and WILLIAM CHILD (died 1699), although, like Purcell, much attracted to secular writing, left some church music which is still performed and still cherished.

SOME MUSIC OF THE SEVENTEENTH CENTURY

Gibbons :	Te Deum from Service in F	Novello
	Deliver us O Lord	Novello
	Drop, drop, slow tears	Stainer & Bell
	This is the record of John	Oxford
Wise :	Awake, up, my glory	Novello
Rogers :	Jubilate from Service in D	Novello
Batten :	Haste thee, O God	Oxford
Humphrey :	Hear, O Heavens	Novello
Blow :	Sing we merrily unto God	Novello
	Let Thy hand	Novello

Purcell :	Rejoice in the Lord alway	Novello
	Remember not, O Lord	Novello
	Thou knowest, Lord	Novello
	Hear my prayer	Novello
	Magnificat and Nunc Dimittis in G minor	
		Novello
Clarke :	Praise the Lord, O Jerusalem	Novello
Child :	O Blessed Jesu	Novello

Some Recordings

Gibbons :	Three-fold Amen	H.M.V. RG 13
Purcell :	Hear my, Prayer	H.M.V. RG 8
Purcell :	Rejoice in the Lord alway	
		Columbia DB 500

VII. THE EIGHTEENTH CENTURY

After the death of Purcell there is a growing gap in English music — filled largely by an influx of foreign musicians : an ever-increasing flood which established the sense of inferiority in British music for the next 170 years. Handel, who was ten years old at Purcell's death, was to be the greatest of these invaders, and a very mixed blessing for English music. His massive religious writings however are not part of our present national story, although of course, many pieces of his oratorios have a permanent place in our church repertory.

This was a great age of opera ; most of it Italianised, and much in doubtful taste. Typical and indicative of the times was the growing popularity of that black sheep of musical art—the virtuoso singer. With church music only a few names appear throughout the century to maintain a declining tradition.

WILLIAM CROFT (died 1727) and MAURICE GREENE (died 1755) were foremost in the early years. The former will be long remembered for his hymn-tunes St. Anne ("O God our help") and Hanover ("O Worship the King"), but both produced many anthems and service-settings which are heard to-day, and still worth hearing. Scholarly and attractive as these are, they frequently lack vitality and personal depth of feeling. The range too, is far narrower than Purcell's, although occasionally, as in Greene's "Lord, let me know mine end," the greater man's work is well maintained.

WILLIAM BOYCE, quite a considerable composer, showed a grace and lightness of touch which will keep his name alive in church music, as it will live outside for his composition of "Heart of Oak." He, at all events, was aware of the tragedy which neglect was bringing to a wonderful tradition. Thanklessly completing the work begun by Greene, he published his Cathedral Music—four volumes of the best sacred music of the previous two centuries. When Boyce died in 1779, there was darkness indeed in the English choral art.

Nevertheless, there was one redeeming feature of this century. As the hymn and the Anglican chant grew in popularity, it was on these very miniature forms of composition that the whole reputation of eighteenth-century music virtually rests. The Hymn-tunes and chants of CROFT, GREENE and BOYCE, together with those of BATTISHILL, TOPLADY, WATTS, and many others within and outside the established church, frequently achieve perfection, and our hymnals and psalters would be much the poorer without them.

There was indeed a tendency for all music—including the larger church forms—to become hymn-like in conception. The composers of anthems employ largely a note-for-syllable style, with voice-parts moving chiefly in chordal sequence— a great contrast to the intricate texture of the earlier polyphony. Such music is not necessarily inferior to any other, but has obvious restrictions in breadth and variety of expression. The work of ill-equipped imitators of Handel, combining with this natural tendency, became increasingly uninspired and lifeless.

But English music could not hope to thrive in such a century. It was a period of wit and finery in the cities (and of unspeakable squalor in the country) : an age of the coffee-house which produced poets like Prior, Gay and Pope — poets whose great lack was that depth of human feeling that

produces good music : a self-satisfied era which considered
Shakespeare an uncouth yokel, and sought its pleasures in
shallow imitations of the ancients. The masterpieces of
Byrd, Farrant, Gibbons and Purcell had no place in such
a society and were forgotten. A sad century indeed for
church music, made sadder by the thought of Haydn's and
Mozart's work in the same period.

SOME MUSIC OF THE EIGHTEENTH CENTURY

Croft :	God is gone up	
	Te Deum from Service in A	
Greene :	Lord, let me know mine end	
	Let God arise	
	Thou visitest the earth	Novello
Boyce :	Save me O God	
	By the waters of Babylon	
	Lord, what is man	
	Te Deum in C	

VIII. THE NINETEENTH CENTURY

The century opened with no improvement. The old
patronage for church composers was gone, and increasing
public audiences tempted composers to write profitable secular
trivialities. Mediocre imitations of Handel's choral music
became the established church fashion.

ATTWOOD (1765–1838) and CROTCH (1775–1847) however
are rightly recalled in the continued use of their anthems
and service-settings. Attwood was an esteemed pupil of
Mozart, and later a friend of Mendelssohn, with whom the
"second Handel" lived for a while. JOHN GOSS and WILLIAM
WALMISLEY were worthy successors, but restricted by the
low creative vitality of the age.

The works of these four men are unpretentious, but
they have a high degree of dignity, charm and appropriateness that justifies their continued popularity.

SAMUEL WESLEY was capable of much fine work, and
his son SAMUEL SEBASTIAN is still justly heard—and com-

DR. JOHN BLOW (1649-1708)

HENRY PURCELL (1658-1695)

mendable for his long and gallant fight against the church authorities for their neglect of music and musicians. HENRY SMART (1810–1879) and W. T. BEST (1826–97) had a pureness of quality that keeps their work alive. STAINER (1840–1901) and STERNDALE BENNETT (1816–75) would have been considerable composers in any other age, but FREDERICK OUSELEY is more often heard now, having avoided many of the sugary pitfalls into which they fell, and showing at least a sense of pure craftsmanship.

Surveying the first seventy years of the nineteenth century is a disheartening task—not so much that the composers we have mentioned were limited in their achievements, but because the remainder, a far larger number, were so artistically perverted, and had such a wide following. The publication of *Hymns Ancient and Modern* in 1861 probably places the whole temper of the century : a certain amount of creditable scholarship, but marred time and time again by squeamish sentimentality. STAINER, DYKES and MONK were among its foremost contributors, and better than many.

The reasons for this poor state of church music:—

1. The previous century had little of value to pass on.

2. The industrial revolution had made Britain more interested in money than the arts.

3. The church itself was completely disinterested in music, and often very corrupt and lax in administration.

4. Some of the Nonconformist " revivals " had incorporated the cheapest of sentimental and emotional music in their evangelism.

5. Imitators of Mendelssohn continued the imitators-of-Handel tradition.

SOME MUSIC OF THE NINETEENTH CENTURY

Attwood :	Magnificat and Nunc Dimittis in C	Novello
	Turn Thy face	Novello
Crotch :	Comfort, O Lord	Bosworth
	How dear are Thy counsels	Novello

Goss :	Service in A	Novello
	I will magnify thee	Novello
	Come, and let us return	Novello
Walmisley :	Magnificat and Nunc Dimittis in D minor	
		Novello
	From all that dwell	Novello
S. S. Wesley :	Wash me throughly	Novello
Smart :	The Lord is my Shepherd	Novello
	Be glad, O ye righteous	Novello
Ouseley :	Service in D	Novello
	O Lord, Thou art my God	Novello

Some Recordings

Walmisley :	Nunc Dimittis in D minor	
		H.M.V. B 9308
Walmisley :	Magnificat in D minor	Columbia 9147
S. S. Wesley :	Thou wilt keep him	H.M.V. RG 9

IX.   THE ENGLISH REVIVAL (1870 onwards)

The dawn broke before the century was through. HUBERT PARRY (1848–1918), C. V. STANFORD (1852–1924) and C. H. LLOYD (1849–1919) produced, almost suddenly, music which was once again worthy of the old heritage of Tallis, Byrd, Gibbons , and Purcell. Slowly the British people began to regain a taste for something better than Stainer's *The Crucifixion,* and its lesser counterparts.

Typical of this new era is Parry's *Blest Pair of Sirens,* a perfect eight-part setting of Milton's perfect poem. It is a superbly sustained piece of polyphonic writing with a great freshness and sincerity in its thrilling climaxes.

A good example of Stanford's work is his service-setting in C major. The opening bars of the Magnificat are like the sudden drawing aside of curtains, letting in pure sunlight where the musty dimness of Victorianism recently reigned.

Lloyd, sound though not spectacular, still finds frequent place in our services.

The awakening, of course, was part of a national stirring of mind and spirit. With the approach of the new century there grew up something akin in spirit to the expansive and inspiring years of the Tudor monarchs.

Musically there were many factors of the times having particular influence:

1. There was a sharp rise in the efficiency of church and cathedral organisation following the work of the Oxford Movement, and of individual agitators.

2. The old national and cathedral festivals were given new vitality, and new ones were established.

3. The great national schools of music appeared in their present form in the seventies. As with the universities, the standard of teaching soon rose to a commendable level.

4. The revival of interest in folk-song had almost as stimulating an effect on church music as it had on secular forms.

5. The scholarship and research of men like E. H. Fellowes and Kennedy Scott rescued much of our past heritage from oblivion and reinstated it in the church's ceremonies.

6. Many of the new composers wrote splendid organ music which enriched our services, and replaced the Victorian sentimental voluntaries, with their successions of dominant sevenths and tremulant waverings.

7. The enlargement of general education after 1870 gradually led to a more discriminating and appreciative congregation.

8. The publication of improved hymnals and psalters.

The full extent of this veritable renaissance can best be shown by listing some of the other chief names of this new English school. They are given in chronological order with the decades in which they were born

1850–60 Edward Elgar, Basil Harwood.

1860–70 W. G. Alcock, Alfred Hollins, Granville Bantock, Richard Terry, Charles Wood, Walford Davies, Tertius Noble.

1870–80 Percy Buck, Vaughan Williams, Edward Bairstow,
Harvey Grace, Gustav Holst, Sydney Nicholson,
Martin Shaw, Roger Quilter, Thomas Dunhill,
Rutland Boughton, Stanley Roper, Harry Farjeon,
Frank Bridge, John Ireland, Geoffrey Shaw.

1880 onwards W. H. Harris, George Dyson, H. G. Ley,
Herbert Howells, Harold Darke, R. O. Morris,
Thomas Wood, E. J. Moeran, Percy Whitlock,
Ernest Bullock, Eric Thiman, and many others.

Among these names are many who in larger fields of the
choral and orchestral art gave Britain once again an international pride in her music. Collectively, and with other
purely secular writers, they form beyond doubt the healthiest
and most virile national school of composers in present times.

Up to the age of Purcell, music had chiefly existed in
the smaller forms such as the church service provided. To-
day the range is infinitely wider and more attractive. However, many of this new English school found their training-
ground in church composition, and not a few have discovered
in it their specialised medium. Althought faults are present
in their work, none has suffered from those lapses in taste
and craftsmanship which preceding decades so misguidedly
applauded. **All have added appreciably to the glorious
tradition of English church music.**

X. THE TWENTIETH CENTURY

The full story of these great achievements belongs to
the present century. Before a quarter of it was passed the
tide of fine new church music was at the flood, and although
composers tend more and more towards the bigger forms in
music, there is no reason to suppose that this new peak in
English church writing has been passed with the approach
of the half-century.

All our present church music is not perfect. Much of it
still has traces of the academic flavour of lesser ages. How-

ever, as at previous points in history, the steady influx of lively secular styles can improve it considerably, and expanding public interest in secular music will have an increasing effect. Good and living music in the church will be demanded by future congregations.

The church, rightly and of necessity, is slow to change. And although it has been often tardy in receiving these valuable new gifts, considerable progress has been made, and at least the larger religious institutions are to-day as good musically as they ever were. Where churches still remain backward, however, the fault is certainly a local one due to their own insufficiency. The Royal School of Church Music, founded in 1928 by Sir Sydney Nicholson, has given further opportunity for the new (and the best of the old) music to spread throughout the land.

The present chapter has recalled two recurrent historical problems which may appear still unsolved.

1. The danger of highly specialised music is discouraging congregations from active participation in the services.

2. The extent to which secular influences are desirable.

From our study of the past and present, however, the answer is near at hand :

1. We can expect congregations to "lag behind" a progressive movement in church music; but that lag will become ever shorter as musical and general education advances.

2. Secular influences are always welcomed if they bring with them something of that art which elevates the spirit. Everything that is best should find its place in church music.

In any case the church service wisely provides for all manner of men. The division of services into choral and congregational elements, as at present, is admirable, and has complete precedent in the earlier climaxes of English music. But let also the simple congregational parts, the hymns, responses, and chanting be vital and (consequently) artistic. There is nothing to prevent their being equally as inspiring as an anthem sung in the chancel.

Some Music of the New English Era

Parry :	My soul, there is a country	Deane & Sons
	Hear my words	Novello
	Service in D major	Novello
Stanford :	Be merciful	Stainer & Bell
	Service in C	Stainer & Bell
Walford Davies :	King of Glory	Curwen
	God be in my head	Novello
Elgar :	Fear not, O land	Novello
	Doubt not thy Father's care	Novello
Vaughan	Benedicite	Oxford
Williams :	Let us now praise famous men	Curwen
Holst :	Festival Te Deum	Stainer & Bell
	Christmas Day	Novello
G. Shaw :	Dawn draws on	Novello
	The spacious firmament	Edward Arnold
Dyson :	Three Songs of Praise	Novello
	Valour	Edward Arnold
Darke :	Benedictus in F major	Stainer & Bell
Kitson :	How sweet the Name	Stainer & Bell
Bullock :	Give us the wings of faith	Oxford
Howells :	Here is the little door	Stainer & Bell
Thiman :	O Lord, support us	Novello
Whitlock :	Communion Service	Oxford

Some Recordings

Stanford :	Gloria in Excelsis	H.M.V. RG 12-13
Stanford :	Te Deum	H.M.V. C 3448-9
Stanford :	Magnificat in G	Columbia 9147
Walford Davies-		
Attwood :	Magnificat	H.M.V. B 9308
Walford Davies :	Be strong	H.M.V. RG 7
Walford Davies :	O little town of Bethlehem	
Vaughan		H.M.V. B 4285
Williams :	Kyrie in G minor	H.M.V. DB 1786
Vaughan		
Williams :	Te Deum	H.M.V. RG 13-14
Bullock :	The Lord send you help	Decca R 001
Bullock		
(arranged)) :	Veni Creater (plainsong hymn)	
		H.M.V. RG 4

XI. A FEW OF THE COMPOSERS
AND THEIR MUSIC

Having reviewed in outline the history of our church music, we can now examine some of the representative composers in rather more detail. It has been thought best here to concern ourselves with composers from about 1600 onwards, for the music of earlier periods demands rather more detailed treatment than space will at present allow. An advantage in this method is that it emphasises the continuity of the church tradition in the last four centuries, and brings to notice the small but ever-present stream of worthy music which linked the end of the "Golden Age" to our own times.

Composers represented in this section

Thomas Weelkes	... ...	1576?—1623
Orlando Gibbons	... ...	1583 —1625
Henry Purcell	... ...	1658?—1695
Thomas Attwood	... ...	1765 —1839
Samuel Wesley	... ...	1766 —1837
William Crotch	... ...	1775 —1847
S. S. Wesley	... ...	1810 —1876
T. A. Walmisley	... ...	1814 —1856
C. H. H. Parry	... ...	1848 —1918
R. R. Terry	... ...	1865 —1938
R. Vaughan Williams	...	born 1872

THOMAS WEELKES

Weelkes was born probably in 1576, and died in 1623. He thus lived through a period when secular music in this country—especially the madrigal—was at its full flourish Much that can be said of his work naturally pertains also to his contemporary, Orlando Gibbons—but these two great composers are included here to underline the high merit of the later Reformation music—when the real Englishness in our tradition was becoming increasingly apparent. Weelkes, however, was primarily a secular composer, and probably the greatest of all our madrigal writers : but such of his church music as recent research has brought to light, shows an almost equal degree of mastery.

In his service-settings and anthems Weelkes displays a fine spirit of adventure typical of his day. Perhaps the greatest advance in his work, however, is his use of block harmonic chords and rests to break the continuous flow of the voice-parts. Typical of contemporary composition too, he has a considerable dramatic sense in his culminative crescendos and in his appropriate use of extremes in voice-register; while in the way of innovations—especially in his secular writing—he was considerably ahead of the more famous Gibbons. Although he is so notable as an experimenter, his ultimate worth depends on his wonderful facility in contrapuntal part-writing. Whether five, six or seven parts are employed, there is always present a vigorous vitality. Times not long before, when composers worked hard at the scientific study of fitting parts together seem far distant. Voice-parts are now completely independent and of equal importance ; imitative entries are natural and effective.

Weelkes' massive *Gloria in Excelsis* is, like most of his works, beyond the power of present-day choirs on normal church occasions. The extract here clearly demonstrates the harmonic sequences, the lively imitations, and the complex counterpoint we have previously mentioned. The work is interesting too in that it is in a distinct ternary form—with a glorious contrapuntal *Amen* serving, as it were as a *coda*.

GLORIA IN EXCELSIS.

Sing, my soul, to God.

ANTHEM FOR CHRISTMAS OR OTHER FESTIVALS.

Edited by
EDMUND H. FELLOWES.

THOMAS WEELKES.
1576?-1623

Original a minor third lower.

O.U.P. 17

ORLANDO GIBBONS

Gibbons provides a focal point in English music. The last of the Elizabethans, he consummated the whole development of the art up to his own day, and also pointed the way ahead in many bold and inspiring ways. Of first importance perhaps is the essential Englishness in his conception of musical composition. He not only wrote entirely to English texts, but showed an unmistakably English quality in his actual music—being an obvious fore-runner of Purcell. For the first time to any sustained extent do we see in Gibbons' music a completely personal means of expression. He has even been called a Romantic in his fineness of feeling for words : certainly there is no occurrence with him, as almost invariably with earlier writers, of writing generalised music for a generalised church dogma. This great advance in expressiveness leads to a variety of style which is very new, and as with Weelkes and the later Purcell, we find a contrast of harmonic and contrapuntal passages, contrasts of pitch and voice-combinations, together with freedom and skilful imitation in the part-writing.

Gibbons was born in Oxford in 1583, of a musical family, and was soon caught up in the many musical advances of his times. At the age of 21 he became organist to the Chapel Royal, and in 1623 organist at Westminster Abbey. He also held many court appointments as a teacher. The great musical experiments of the times found a ready patron in Gibbons, and, apart from being the foremost exponent of the organ and virginals, he wrote substantially in all the current forms of composition. His innovations include developments in the "verse-anthem," the introduction of solo parts, and advances with orchestral accompaniments. He was not, however, drawn into trivialities of the day, and fundamentally is well within the main stream of musical development, showing all that was best in the music that preceded him. It was for Purcell to advance these measures still further and to add the more "modern" effect of balance and rhythm within the flow of the counterpoint.

Almighty and Everlasting God shows a similar contrapuntal texture to that of the Weelkes example—but, in keeping with the text is naturally of a more subdued nature.

Tudor Church Music

Published for the

CARNEGIE UNITED KINGDOM TRUST

by the

OXFORD UNIVERSITY PRESS, AMEN HOUSE, E.C.4.

Nº 36.   *Price Twopence.*

Almighty and Everlasting God

Anthem for Four Voices

Edited by
E. H. FELLOWES

ORLANDO GIBBONS
(1583-1625

Original: a minor third lower.

As we usually find with Gibbons however, the flow of part-writing is rather more continuous—and, if anything, has a slightly more formal flavour. For sheer beauty, dignity, and purity of style Gibbons nevertheless surpasses anything that preceded him in our musical history. (The accompaniment, as with the Weelkes example, is of course included by the present editor for practice purposes).

HENRY PURCELL

Purcell was born in London in 1658 or 1659, and although little is known of his earliest years (there are several contradictory accounts) he was certainly born into a musical family with connections at the Chapel Royal—of which he became a chorister at an early age. Pelham Humphrey and John Blow were among his teachers, and Purcell began composing while still a boy. When his voice broke, however, his greatest experience came—for he was given several official appointments, including keeper of the king's wind instruments, copyist, conductor (i.e. harpsichord-player), composer to the king's string band, etc. This varied work, at a time when the art of music was rapidly expanding on the secular side gave the young Purcell fine equipment for his later years.

At the early age of twenty Purcell succeeded Blow as organist at Westminster Abbey—a post which he retained right up to his death—and he began to compose voluminously in all the vocal and instrumental forms of the day. Church music, indeed, claims a relatively minor proportion of Purcell's work, but the many anthems and two service-settings which we sing to-day are of greatest beauty and sincerity. There is a tremendous vigour and zest in his anthems, together with a great variety of style and texture. In his verse and chorus sections he frequently alternates between the flowing polyphonic medium and the newer more fashionable harmonic progressions. His innovations with organ or orchestral accompaniments and interludes are of great interest—although many of his larger orchestral anthems become too long for normal use nowadays. Other points of interest are his extensive employment of violins in his accompaniments—the violin then being considered

14

Purcell's Service in G minor.

vulgar and barbaric beside the more placid viol—and, as we have mentioned earlier, his frequent introduction of solo passages into his choral works. Purcell himself had a fine bass voice, but his many bass solos were written specifically for a member of the Chapel Royal named John Gostling, and their great range makes many of these anthems a rarity to-day. Purcell also sang well as a *falsetto* alto, and here again our present-day performers find Purcell's alto parts very difficult to perform. Purcell used then the whole forces of the art to their fullest extent, and his ingenuity in calling on secular forms and in incorporating any worth-while innovation makes Purcell's contribution to the church's musical history very great indeed.

There are two service-settings of Purcell's in present-day use, and the quotation here is from the *Gloria* of his famous G Minor Service. Harmonic and polyphonic mastery are well in evidence, and we are frequently reminded throughout this work that Purcell could write with great success in the more dramatic forms of music. He also makes fine use of anti-phonal singing (where alternate sides of the chancel sing "verse" passages and then join forces in sections for full choir). This *Gloria* begins with some thrilling canonic writing, and the great variety of Purcell's texture is soon apparent : sustained counterpoint, harmonic sequences and the stimulating interpolation of solo passages all add to its manifold attractions. Above all, there is strength and vigour here which most later composers were quite unable to attain.

THOMAS ATTWOOD

Attwood was quite a prolific composer in many forms of music, but unfortunately could not free himself from the deadening inartistic atmosphere which had descended on eighteenth century England.

Born in Chelsea in 1765, he became a chorister of the Chapel Royal at the age of thirteen. He, like Purcell, had good fortune at the end of his choir-boy career, having the then rare experience of being sent abroad to study under royal patronage—his patron being the Prince of Wales (later George IV). As mentioned in the historical survey, Attwood presents an interesting figure in English music, having been

Turn Thy face from my sins.

ANTHEM.

Psalm li. 9, 10, 11.

Composed by THOMAS ATTWOOD.

LONDON: NOVELLO AND COMPANY, LIMITED

a close friend of both Mozart and Mendelssohn. Whether Attwood really had the makings of greatness in him or not is difficult to say, but the promise he showed under Mozart's tuition in Vienna did not flourish on his return to England— and the capabilities praised by his illustrious teacher came to little. However, although he failed to infuse our music with the polished artistry of Vienna, Attwood holds a creditable place in English musical history. He became an example of those church musicians who, alone in the whole field of our music, produced works sincerely conceived and sound in craftsmanship. He was renowned as a teacher, held many court appointments, and won respect as organist of St. Paul's Cathedral and conductor for the Philharmonic Society. He died in 1838 and was buried in St. Paul's

Our example of Attwood's work, *Turn Thy Face from my sins,* is a "verse" anthem—a form, as we have seen, much favoured by Purcell. (Where the full choir sings throughout a work the term "full anthem" is normally used.) It is still quite well-known to-day, and is rather typical of the dozen or so anthems we have under Attwood's name. Written with a formal organ accompaniment—in which the organ makes no individual contribution—it has in comparison with our previous examples, an over-refinement and a rather forced simplicity which detracts from its artistic power and value. The dominant-seventh harmonies and 4/3 suspensions are too prevalent, giving the work something of a self-righteous atmosphere. The formal repetition of phrases in the text is also rather typical of music of this period. Although we cannot feel, as with composers a century earlier or later, that the composer is speaking with great personal conviction, there remains a certain sincerity and a slender charm in this work that will keep it alive. Its fitness and appropriateness—valuable assets—can be appreciated only on hearing it performed in its proper setting. But we lament the absence of the virile polyphony and bold strong harmony present in Purcell, Gibbons and Weelkes.

SAMUEL WESLEY

Born in Bristol in 1766, Samuel Wesley is not, strictly speaking, a great church composer. The son of Charles

DR. WILLIAM BOYCE (1710-1779)

DR. RALPH VAUGHAN WILLIAMS

IN EXITU ISRAEL.

Wesley the hymn-writer, he became a Roman Catholic early in his career, and thus his purely church music is limited in extent. Much of his time too was spent with secular composition, and with his distinctive function of organ-playing. But for all this, Wesley remains of the very greatest value to the English church tradition—chiefly in his strenuous work to revive the glories of J. S. Bach, a composer virtually unknown in this country at the time. Wesley, the greatest organist of his day, achieved much in this direction, and later was joined by others—including the visiting Mendelssohn. Thus at a time when English music was of very low vitality, Wesley sought guidance from the best possible source, and persuaded many later composers to do the same : the ultimate value of this work to English music was perhaps far greater than we realise.

The few of Wesley's motets which survive are not, however, mere imitations of Bach, for, a thorough scholar, he also studied earnestly the works of Byrd and Gibbons—a very rare occurrence in this period. In reviving the polyphonic style too, Wesley added a strong vitality born of his own idealism and sincerity, and drew on the many harmonic and structural resources of his own day.

We quote here from *In Exitu Israel*, a splendid motet for double chorus, and realise that even the rightly maligned nineteenth century could produce *some* really first-rate music —to most people a surprising discovery. It is with such compositions that the church alone sustained the precarious continuity of the art in England. The influences Wesley sought give the work a solid strength and dignity, and the whole is admirably suited to its text from the 114th psalm. In particular is it free from the stinted academic formality which marred most nineteenth-century attempts at polyphony, and from the timidity and self-consciousness of the numerous lesser composers—the composers of "hymn-tune anthems." It is unfortunate that these rare works of Wesley are too lengthy and difficult (being influenced by the oratorioform) for frequent use at present—but they have a permanent place in the repertory of church festival music.

WILLIAM CROTCH

Born in Norwich in 1775, Crotch is an interesting if minor figure in our musical history. His father, a carpenter, built an organ upon which the young Crotch learnt to play at an incredibly early age. He gave recitals in London at the age of four and composed an oratorio before his fifteenth birthday. He took his Bachelor of Music at Oxford, and became Professor of Music there in 1797—achieving great renown as a teacher. His "Elements of Musical Composition" had long and extensive popularity after its publication in 1812.

There is none of Wesley's ardent pioneering about Crotch, and it is interesting to place a good example of his work—the standard type of composition of the day—alongside the greater man's work. We reproduce therefore an extract from his *Comfort, O Lord,* an anthem still frequently sung—and part of a larger work, *Be Merciful unto me.* It is completely un-pretentious, and simple in the extreme, yet it has a serene and mellow quality that raises it well above the commonplace. Many composers of the day made mawkish sentimentality out of such a text, but here Crotch attains a high degree of success. The music is certainly appropriate to both text and function—indeed one can say that the music with its tender and restrained pleading has a distinctly comforting quality. Again our conclusion is that the artistic spirit of the time was not completely extinct while such achievements, slender though they may be, continued to exist.

52

COMFORT, O LORD.
Short Full Anthem
(from "Be Merciful")
by
Dr. W. CROTCH.

Ps. lxxxvi. 4, 6, 11.

Edited by
SIR FREDERICK BRIDGE.

Note. This Edition follows the Composer's Version (1804). Additional words have, however, been thought necessary to avoid the too frequent repetition of the same text.

Copyright Bosworth & Co. 1910.   B. & Co. 148

SAMUEL SEBASTIAN WESLEY

The son of Samuel Wesley was born in London in 1810 and died in Gloucester in 1876. Rarely can a man have lived up to illustrious christian names so fully, or so completely fulfilled his father's hopes! Taking his place alongside the whole range of English composers, S. S. Wesley can unreservedly be called great. A chorister of the Chapel Royal, he showed remarkable early promise at the organ, with which instrument he out-topped his father's fame—serving among other places at Hereford and Gloucester cathedrals.

With the younger Wesley we are aware, probably for the first time, that the English musical tradition is not merely hanging on grimly to life, but looking forward with determination to the future : not that Wesley's musical output was very extensive, nor that it contained any startling innovations which foreshadowed a new era. But the fight is fully joined against the laxity and artistic sterility of the day. Discouraged by lack of support and impoverished choirs, Wesley did not write extensively, but the quality is abundantly and confidently present. Influences from his father, from Bach, and perhaps most of all from Purcell are always evident—together with a fire of personal conviction for the cause he was fighting. Purcell is present in the variety of harmonic and polyphonic styles, the frequent dramatic touches, and the fine arias, while to these Wesley adds a more advanced measure and harmony and a masterly use of recitative. Many of his anthems, like those of his father, are too lengthy for normal church and cathedral use to-day, but the smaller works are well known and widely cherished.

Thou wilt keep him, which we quote here, although one of the slighter works, shows what above all we can expect of Wesley—complete sincerity. It has a few nineteenth-century touches that are well out of favour at present, but it is very pleasing music both to perform and hear—and has a beauty of melody, a dignity, and a complete appropriateness that will keep it alive in our services.

THOU WILT KEEP HIM IN PERFECT PEACE

FULL ANTHEM FOR FIVE VOICES.

COMPOSED BY

SAMUEL SEBASTIAN WESLEY.

Isaiah xxvi 3; Ps. cxxxix 11; 1 John i. 5; Ps. cxix. 175.

LONDON: NOVELLO AND COMPANY, LIMITED; NEW YORK: THE H. W. GRAY CO., SOLE AGENTS FOR THE U.S.A.

THOMAS ATTWOOD WALMISLEY

Walmisley, born in London in 1814, was again the son of a musician, inheriting the best musical environment of the day and soon developing a fine ability at the organ key-board. A pupil and god-son of Attwood, whose name he bears, Walmisley joined those few nineteenth-century composers who looked back to the glories of the past rather than accept the popular sacred music of the day. (One of the chief difficulties that these pioneers had to face was the introduction of cheap choral music-publishing after about 1830. This valuable commercial enterprise came—perhaps inevitably—at the wrong time. Hundreds of mediocre anthems and service-settings flooded the country, and very many of them are still in existence.) Walmisley's high artistic judgement becomes all the more remarkable in this setting, but it is significant that he fought strenuously to revive the purifying influence of Bach and Purcell. He did this to considerable effect while professor of music at Cambridge. He died at the early age of 42.

Walmisley wrote a considerable number of anthems—some of them disappointing to us to-day, but the Victorians were always at their best with service-settings. The anthem-form with its free choice of text, left them too much liberty and frequently led to lapses of taste, lapses from which Walmisley himself was not immune. As an example of Walmisley's writing then, we choose the famous D Minor Service, still a firm favourite with our choirs, and a work conceived with a distinct strength and conviction of utterance. There is no sentimental weakness of melody or harmony, and a notable freedom from the mechanical squareness of phrase and the false accentuation of words which were almost inevitable in contemporary church music. The chording and careful balance of the antiphonal sections remind us strongly of Purcell, although no attempt is made at the older master's complexity of counterpoint. Of considerable interest too, is the organ accompaniment. This is probably the first example of a service-setting having an organ part boldly instrumental and independent of the vocal parts. The whole work is not difficult of execution, but is very satisfying and enjoyable to both singer and listener.

* If there is not much echo in your Church, this Chord is to be played as a Semibreve. Sw. Reed. ♭ ♯

Dr Walmisley's Services.—(No. 2.)

C. HUBERT H. PARRY

In some respects Sir Hubert Parry was similar to many of his musical predecessors. He was born into a musical family (1848) and was a man of varied gifts and capabilities. He was too, a man of great personal charm, a thorough scholar, and a youthful prodigy. The elements of his life and career, therefore, could be those of many we have mentioned earlier, but these attributes came nearly a hundred years later than they did, for example, in Attwood, and through them the late blossoming of English music—long hoped for by those we have been discussing—became a reality.

Parry, with every environmental aid, qualified as an Oxford Bachelor of Music while still at Eton, and made his first significant contribution to musical literature at the Gloucester Festival of 1880. His appointment as professor at the newly-established Royal College of Music in 1883 hampered his early zeal for composition, but towards the end of the century this great sportsman-artist was producing choral works of the greatest power and originality. Large oratorical compositions, instrumental music of many kinds, part and solo songs, all followed rapidly, and—perhaps most important of all—the public were now ready to receive once again music worthy of our old traditions. Throughout Parry's work there is a natural and robust forcefulness of style : a harmonic, contrapuntal and even dramatic mastery : a spaciousness and craftsmanship which has few traces of the academic self-consciousness of all but the best of earlier composers. Above all there is a pure Englishness of style which was to find fuller and more comprehensive expression when it descended to the greater genius of Elgar.

A great teacher, Parry is still frequently recalled in his musical writings—some of which, like his "Evolution of the Art of Music" and "Studies of Great Composers" are invaluable to the student to this day. He was knighted in 1898, and succeeded Stainer as Professor of Music at Oxford in 1901. Dying at the age of seventy, widely respected and admired in himself and his work, he was buried in St. Paul's Cathedral.

My Soul, there is a Country is typical of Parry's smaller choral works. Although appropriate to church use and

Motet.

"My soul, there is a country."

for the group called

"SONGS OF FAREWELL."

Words by
HENRY VAUGHAN.

Music by
C. HUBERT H. PARRY.

frequently on the cathedral lists, it contains an invigorating element of the secular part-song, and a certain lyrical quality : it has a freshness, vitality and consummate artistry which give it a universal value and appeal. Like most modern composers, Parry shows impeccable choice of words for his vocal settings, and here he uses every fine shade of thought and emotion to the full. There is a great variety of style in the easy-flowing polyphony and the sudden dramatic chordal sequences. It is a composition of rare beauty, and sung (unaccompanied) in its proper setting, achieves all we can ask of church music.

RICHARD R. TERRY

Sir Richard Terry, like many musicians throughout our history, was not primarily a church composer, although his contributions to the church repertory are highly valued.

Terry was born in 1865 and died in London in 1938. He thus covers a most interesting period of musical development. Becoming Director of Music at Westminster Roman Catholic Cathedral, he was a modern example of the scholar-musician, and left many fine critical writings on music. However, the name of Richard Terry is probably most widely known to the general public in connection with folk-song of the sea—namely shanties—where his collecting and editing made a distinctive and valuable contribution to our musical literature. Terry was, in fact, a very great authority on folk-song of all kinds, and made notable researches into Tudor and medieval music. It is appropriate therefore that we include here an example of the folk-song of the church—the carol, to represent his work.

Our quotation is from one of the twelve delightful carols by this composer, and is well representative. The scholarship and idealism of men of this school has led to an accuracy and care in their approach to music which has been invaluable to our present musical knowledge. Among the mass of nineteenth-century church compositions we have mentioned were many inferior tunes (with equally inferior words) published under the title of "carols." Terry, however, insists that merely because the words are appropriate to Christmas, it does not follow that they become a carol when

MYN LYKING.

R.R.TERRY

set to music, but rather "a tune can only be termed a carol the nearer it approximates to the folk-song type, and the farther it departs from the hymn-tune."

Using words of fourteenth-century origin, Terry thus recaptures the true traditional spirit of the carol, and at the same time gives us something of great beauty, purity, and sincerity. Of its kind nothing could be more pleasurable to sing, and here is one example of many modern works of great merit which can be well rendered by any good amateur choir. The part quoted includes the chorus—a distinctive feature of the carol-form.

RALPH VAUGHAN WILLIAMS

It is quite impossible to name any one modern composer as representative of present-day church composition. Styles are widely varied and a high degree of artistic achievement is apparent on many sides.

Dr. Vaughan Williams was born in Gloucestershire in 1872, and received a full academic musical education. From 1890 to 1896 he studied under Stanford, Parry and Charles Wood, and thus became well versed in the new English tradition. A period of work abroad under Max Bruch and Maurice Ravel no doubt added a spirit of experiment and adventure to this sound nurture. But the distinctive force in his music derives from his intense study of English folksong and music of the Tudor period—a study which resulted not in the amassing of academic knowledge, but in the resurrection of the true living spirit of this early music.

This is no place to discuss the great merits of this composer, or to dwell on his contributions to the major orchestral and choral forms of music. In his smaller vocal and choral works however he achieves equal success—sometimes through the medium of the earlier English schools, and sometimes (as in the example quoted) more in the Englishness of the Parry-Elgar tradition. The extract is a unisonsong setting of a fine passage from Ecclesiasticus XLIV, and although writing in this miniature form the composer achieves a moving dignity of spirit—indeed even a splendour in music, which has given this work a prominent place in our churches, cathedrals, and schools, for ceremonial occasions.

Let us now praise famous men.

R. VAUGHAN WILLIAMS

The passage commences soon after a sudden change from the key of E major to E flat, where, after grandly singing of the glories of the famous, we recall the virtue—and equality—of those whose names are not enscrolled in great historical records. The massive measured tread of the bass figure moves on relentlessly throughout the work, like the passing of time itself. The bold changes in harmony, the strong challenging discords, the fluency and complete appropriateness of the melody add up to a tremendous strength of expression. As with hundreds of other modern examples of church music which could be cited, we feel that the "Golden Age" of English music has at long last returned.

XI. SOME BOOKS FOR FURTHER READING

Title	*Author*	*Publisher*
History of English Music	H. Davey	Curwen
The Glory of English Music	Basil Maine	Wilmer
Music in England	E. Blom	Penguin
English Cathedral Music	E. H. Fellowes	Methuen
English Church Composers	W. A. Barrett	Sampson Low
A History of Music in England	E. Walker	Oxford
Manual of English Church Music	Gardner and Nicholson	S.P.C.K.
Voice and Verse	H. C. Colles	Oxford
The Progress of Music	G. Dyson	Oxford
A Short History of Music	A. Einstein	Cassell
Summary of Musical History	C. H. H. Parry	Novello
The Growth of Music (Parts I & III)	H. C. Colles	Oxford

Title	Author	Publisher
The Listener's Guide to Music	P. Scholes	Oxford
The Complete Book of the Great Musicians	P. Scholes	Oxford
Cameos of Musical History	S. Macpherson	Boosey
William Byrd	Frank Howes	Kegan Paul
William Byrd	E. H. Fellowes	Oxford
Purcell	J. A. Westrup	Dent
Henry Purcell	W. H. Cummings	Sampson Low
Purcell	A. K. Holland	Bell
John Blow	H. Watkins Shaw	Hinrichsen
The Puritans and Music	P. Scholes	Oxford
English Madrigal Composers	E. H. Fellowes	Oxford
Music and Worship	Harvey Grace	Novello
Music and Religion	B. Wibberley	Epworth
The Story of Organ Music	Abdy Williams	Scott
The Story of Notation	Abdy Williams	Scott
Hymnody Past and Present	C. S. Phillips	S.P.C.K.
Musical Instruments and their Music	G. R. Hayes	Oxford
Modern Music and Musicians	W. McNaught	Novello

Oxford History of Music (Introductory Volume and relevant later chapters)

Relevant Articles in :

    Grove's Dictionary of Music and Musicians
    Musical Articles from Encyclopædia Britannica (Tovey)
    Oxford Companion to Music (Scholes)
    Hinrichsen's Musical Year Book (Vols. 1 to III)

Relevant Journals :

    English Church Music, Musical Opinion, Musical Times, The Choir, The Organ.